Yvette Greslé is a writer and art historian based in London. Her endeavours relate to the transformative and political possibilities of the moving image and writing as memory work. She is a Research Associate with the University of Johannesburg.

Unearthed is typeset in Sabon. A characteristic feature of this typeface, designed by Jan Tschichold in the mid 1960s, is that the *italics* take up exactly the same space as the roman.

GW00642982

Unearthed

Yvette Greslé

Copy Press

The Copy Press Limited
51 South Street
Ventnor
Isle of Wight
PO38 1NG

copypress.co.uk

Commune no. 13
Editor: Yve Lomax
Reader: Vit Hopley
Copy-editor: Sara Peacock
Design: Opal Morgen/John Peacock

Front cover © Yvette Greslé

Printed on Munken Print White
no.18 80gsm. Munken Print White
standard products are FSCTM
and PEFC certified.

Printed and bound in England.

First edition © Copy Press Ltd/
Yvette Greslé, 2019

Yvette Greslé asserts the moral right
to be identified as the author of
this work.

A catalogue record for this book is
available from the British Library

ISBN-13   978-1-909570-06-1

For Nicholas and my mother Sylvia

Madame Blanche lived at the White House
White House near the market
Madame Blanche
lived at the White House
she always seen
watering flowers

she haunt people at night
in their bed
she follow them close
up the stairs
rush after them
up the wooden stairs

(Hazel de Silva, '*Madame* Blanche', Sega of Seychelles)

Contents

Swamp

What's the swamp? The swamp is a feeling. It's a feeling of being stuck. The first time the inside of my head felt like a swamp I was eleven years old; it was 1982. Today, I'm stuck in the swamp and remembering that first time. Then I was living somewhere else. Now I live in London. Before that, I lived in Johannesburg. Before that, I lived on Mahé Island, part of the Seychelles archipelago. People have often asked me where the Seychelles are. They say they have never heard of them. If they have, the image they hold in their mind is one of postcard exoticism. *Why would you leave such a beautiful place?*

The islands are located in the Indian Ocean, just south of the equator, in the eastern and southern hemispheres, north-east of Madagascar and east of

Kenya. Most people live on Mahé Island, which is called the main island. The second largest island is Praslin. While anyone can travel easily to many of the islands in proximity to Mahé, other islands are less accessible. The islands closer to Mahé are called the Inner Islands and those further out are known as the Outer Islands. The Inner Islands are granitic and the Outer are coralline although this mapping is not without ambiguity. The Seychelles are comprised of well over 100 islands and I can't say with any scientific accuracy how many there are as the numbers keep shifting. New islands have been dredged up from the seabed and reclaimed from the ocean. The last count of islands I read was 163. Dense mangrove forests once edged Mahé coastlines and there were also crocodiles, which were hunted and killed by settlers. The mangroves have mostly been cleared away. Mahé is also where Victoria, the capital named after Queen Victoria, is located. We call the capital 'town'. In 1900, a statue of Queen Victoria was unveiled in town to celebrate her Diamond Jubilee. The statue, which is tiny, is atop a ceramic fountain and I have heard that passers-by mistake it for the Virgin Mary and cross themselves as they walk past.

At this moment, I'm eleven years old and I'm sitting next to my mother in my great-aunt's sitting room, in Anse Royale on the south-eastern coast of Mahé. The room looks out onto a garden. From the garden there's a road. Cross the road and there's a beach overlooking the Indian Ocean. A coral reef separates the bay from the ocean. In the bay, on the far left-hand side, facing the sea, there is a small granitic island with rocks and a few trees. More accurately, it's an islet because it's so tiny and can be walked around in no time at all. It's called Rat Island. I don't know how it got its name and I have never actually seen any rats there. I did try to swim to it but I got caught in a current and was almost swept out to sea. Rat Island is close to a series of small beaches separated by granite rocks and foliage. The beaches are called Fairyland. The coral reef keeps sharks out of the bay although once while I was swimming at Fairyland my brother started shouting: 'Sharks! Sharks!' I thought he was just trying to scare me but then I saw them. *They were only baby sharks.* In the bay at Anse Royale there is a gap in the reef through which fishing boats travel out to the open sea. We call it The Pass. I have seen a hammerhead shark there and rays that swoop out of the water and back down again.

The beach, across the road from my great-aunt's house, is long and the sand is soft and white. The sea changes from season to season. In the monsoon months the water becomes choppy and murky. Seaweed washes up onto the shore. The seaweed, which is golden-brown when wet, has miniature balloon-like forms that I like to pop between my fingers. It clusters at the point at which waves break into the sand, scratching my skin as I dive into the water. At other times of the year, the water is crystal clear and warm, too warm. When it's full moon, it's like a mirror. I know every inch of the bay, where to swim, where there are underwater worlds of coral, seaweed, shells, shifting sands and fish. When I go diving for shells, I find cowries hidden in the crevices beneath corals. Cowrie shells are smooth and shiny and when I hold them in the palm of my hand they gleam in the sunlight. Cowries are marine molluscs. They are living things. Sometimes I dive for cone shells and when I find them I bring them up to the surface of the water carefully because the snails that live inside them are poisonous. I bury the shells in the ground until the snails inside them die and then I wash them and add them to my collection. At Fairyland, I put on a mask and dive down to the corals to get to the lion fish, which are beautiful in form, shape and pattern. They have fan-like fins and spines that move with the water as they hover beneath corals. I am afraid of being stung by their spines yet I am compelled to swim up to them. Afterwards, I float on the water and look towards the ocean. It extends to a distant horizon line, which is mysterious, and I long to see beyond it.

The front door of my great-aunt's house, which also leads straight into the sitting room, is always open to let in a breeze. The room is long and narrow and circled with chairs. There are wooden chairs with rattan backs and seats with ornamental arms and feet. There are also plantation chairs of the kind that fathers and grandfathers would sleep on with legs stretched out after Sunday lunch. My favourite chair has twisted arms and legs. It has engravings on the back. The engravings are of flowers.

I put down my glass of icy orange squash and put a sweet into my mouth. The sweet is pale yellow and when I bite into it the inside is sherbet. It tastes lemony and acidic. The flavours catch at the back of my throat. I cough and move around in my chair. My body is heavy. My back presses into the hardness of the wood. My arms weigh down into the arm-rests. I'm waiting for something. I don't know what it is I'm waiting for. I'm longing for something. I don't know what it is I'm longing for. I feel as though I've lost something, but I don't know what it is I've lost. I feel a weight. It's like those seconds after a nightmare. You don't know where you are. Half awake, still in a dream.

My mother is looking ahead through the louvred windows towards the garden, the road and the sea. She's fanning herself with one of the fans my great-aunt gives her visitors. I also have a fan. It's resting on my lap. It's hot. It's always hot. Sweat gathers on my forehead and at the back of my neck. My hair feels damp. It hangs long between my shoulder blades in a dark brown plait. There is a lithograph of a young Napoleon on the wall behind my mother and me. Soon his image will be absorbed into the dampness. 'I feel depressed.' I don't know how I know the word. 'Nonsense', my mother says. 'Go for a swim.' I can't move. I can't lift myself off my chair.

The air is thick with tension. Insults are flung care-lessly to and fro. The island is silent. Thoughts echo backwards and forwards. In the heat of yet another Sunday afternoon, I fall asleep on the chaise longue next to my great-aunt's chair. The chaise longue is heavy and Victorian; its velvet upholstery far too hot. I am awoken by an atmosphere, a sensation of heaviness. It feels like the atmospheres human beings create when they're not very happy about something; the kind that fills a room and leaves everyone shifting in their chairs. People say you can cut it with a knife.

Behind my great-aunt's house, which is on a plateau, there are other houses in-between thick vegetation. It's always so hot and sticky and at dusk, mosquitos buzz around my ears. They irritate me and I start smacking at my ears with the palms of my hands. Sometimes, one lands on my arm and I smack it hard. I wipe away the blood and see the mosquito's remains in the palm of my hand. Whenever they bite, little red bumps form on my skin and I can't stop scratching. The more I scratch the more they itch. In one of the houses crockery started to fly around, for no reason at all. My great-aunt walked in with her rosary and it all stopped and went silent. I didn't actually see this with my own eyes. But the story has been repeated to me over and over again. Now, sit-ting on my favourite chair, half in the room and half in the swamp, I see my great-aunt out of the corner of my eye. She sits in this room, in the same white rattan chair, minute by minute, hour by hour, day by day. Her hands are white and smooth. She uses them to fan herself with a rattan fan or edges her fingers along the mother-of-pearl beads of her rosary. She has dark eyes and hair streaked with grey. She is neither tall nor slim. She wears dresses made of fabrics that are variously plain or printed with some kind of floral pattern. They have short sleeves, collars and buttons down the front. Around my great-aunt's neck is a thick gold chain with a Mother and Child pendant. My great-aunt never married, but I have heard the grown-ups mention a lost love. When I visit her with my mother she tells us about her maladies and pains. When I tell my mother about my maladies and pains she tells me that I am like my great-aunt. She says I am a hypochondriac. She says my great-aunt is a hypochondriac.

My great-aunt's name is Tante Hoppy and she lives in her house with Nan Nan Alda. Nan Nan Alda sleeps in a room off the kitchen. Tante Hoppy sleeps on the opposite side of the house from Nan Nan Alda; next to her bedroom is another bedroom and a bathroom. Neither Nan Nan Alda nor Tante Hoppy speaks English. One day, I arrive to visit them early in the morning. Hoppy is sitting at the table in the middle of the kitchen eating toast and jam. Nan Nan Alda had made her breakfast and a pot of vanilla tea. The tea that is produced on the island is drunk with tinned carnation milk. Tante Hoppy is sitting down and Nan Nan Alda is standing up. Nan Nan Alda is wearing a long skirt with a floral pattern, a white blouse and a headscarf. Like Tante Hoppy she is neither tall nor slim but while Tante Hoppy's skin is white hers is black. I watch Tante Hoppy pour her tea into her saucer to cool it then pour it back from the saucer into the cup. They laugh as I stand there watching them. They speak to each other in French. I speak to them in broken French.

Tante Hoppy belonged to the island world of the landowners and planters. Nan Nan Alda belonged to the island world of the people who arrived as the enslaved. Tante Hoppy, like my father, was born on Mahé Island, a descendant of French settlers. The Seychelles were first settled, in any permanent sense, in 1770 after which, in the aftermath of the Napoleonic wars, they became British. After a period of being administered from the island of Mauritius, which was also ceded to Britain, the Seychelles became a British crown colony in 1903. On 28 August 1833, the British Parliament passed the act for the abolition of slavery but while slave owners received economic compensation the slaves received nothing. Slavery was abolished in Seychelles in 1835. The descendants of the French settlers kept their land and their language. The descendants of the enslaved kept on working on the plantations. When I was a child, the histories of the slaves, their ancestors and their descendants were largely unspoken. Someone might say something but only in passing. *Nan Nan Alda is the descendant of slaves.* I knew the family names of the descendants of French colonists. I didn't know the family names of the people descended from the slaves, and their first names were all French. Sometimes there was a glimpse of something. A space would open and then close. *Sensations. Feelings. Something is buried. I can sense it but I can't see it.*

French and English were the languages of white domination and when I was a child French and English were considered linguistically, culturally and socially superior to Creole. Creole is the language that emerged directly from the experience of slavery and the forcible displacement of people from disparate parts of the world through the dynamics of European colonialism, trade and empire. The language I heard around me the most growing up was Creole even though I was never encouraged to speak it. *Mon ale* (I go). *Mon pe ale* (I am going). *Mon'n ale* (I have gone). *Mon ti ale* (I went). *Mon pou ale* (I will go). Later, there would be a movement to write down the Seychellois Creole language, known as Kreol or Seselwa.

My European ancestors were determined to see all kinds of superiority in European-ness and whiteness and all kinds of inferiority in African-ness and blackness. *Were there any exceptions to this narrative?* I have never encountered any. Racism, and the gradations of every kind of prejudice and dominance, has always been a part of my life. It has always been there in all its mundanity and ordinariness. I have seen things with my own eyes. I have heard things with my own ears. I am a witness to its ordinariness.

When racism or any kind of prejudice is subtle only the person it's aimed at knows that it's happening. Maybe the person doing the aiming knows what they're doing or maybe they pretend not to know or maybe they bury their knowing because, after all, there are good whites and bad whites. I grew up accepting the ordinariness of who cleaned the house and who tended the garden. I grew up with the ordinariness of the colonial order of things and the banality of apartheid in the spaces where other whites, like me, lived. It has taken me a long time to unpick the ordinariness of things that are unjust. (It will take me until the end of my life to unpick ordinary things.)

My father spoke French, Creole and English. He is now dead. My mother is South African and she speaks Afrikaans and English. Afrikaans is the language associated with white Afrikaner nationalism and apartheid oppression. At the same time, it is not only spoken by white Afrikaners and has a complex relationship to people who, while oppressed by colonialism, slavery and apartheid, contributed to the formation of the language (its lexicon, its idiomatic expressions and other inflections such as how a word might be pronounced). The texture and rhythm of the language also depends on your cultural references and which part of South Africa you are from. Historians say that Afrikaans has been influenced by Dutch settlers at the Cape; indigenous people, the Khoikhoi and the San; and seafarer variants of Malay,

Portuguese and Indonesian languages. *Piesang means banana (derived from Malay). Sambreel means umbrella (derived from Portuguese). Gogga means bug (derived from Khoikhoi).*

In 1984, when I was thirteen years old, my parents sent me to an English-speaking boarding school in Johannesburg. Everyone had to learn Afrikaans and I was put in the class for immigrants. At the boarding school, I would be asked: 'Are you Portuguese, Italian, Greek, Israeli, Indian or Coloured?' In apartheid South Africa, Coloured is the name given to people who, it was decided, were mixed-race or not white enough. When I tell people who aren't white this story later in life they are surprised and they say: 'But you look white to me.'

After my parents were engaged some of the people my mother knew asked her why a nice Afrikaner girl would marry a foreigner. And when I was born in Johannesburg, Dr Rothschild asked my mother why she gave birth to a Chinese baby. When my father left Seychelles on a ship to go to university in Cape Town in the 1950s, the South African authorities requested a letter from the Bishop of Seychelles. In the letter, the Bishop was to confirm my father's race. *It was important to say that he was white.*

Zimitri Erasmus, a South African scholar from Cape Town, writes about her relationship to the South African category Coloured. Her words draw attention to the psychological effects of racism and its absurd but pernicious ideology. *'For me, growing up coloured meant knowing that I was not only not white, but less than white, not only not black, but better than black (as we referred to African people) ... The humiliation of being "less than white" made being "better than black" a very fragile position to occupy. The pressure to be respectable and to avoid shame created much anxiety.'*

When I was a child I had a fight with my Seychelloise grandmother. She insisted that I come out of the sun. I refused. I started telling her things. I can't remember exactly what I said. But I do remember that what I said must have been bad because my father was angry and I felt ashamed. Perhaps my grandmother wanted me to get out of the sun because I might get sunstroke. Or perhaps she wanted me to get out of the sun because she didn't want my skin to get too dark. She and Tante Hoppy were sisters. Whenever they went out into the sun they carried a parasol or wore a hat. My grandmother developed Alzheimer's and her memories got all muddled up. I sit next to her in Tante Hoppy's sitting room and we each hold a fan. I fan myself with mine and she holds hers in her lap. She begins to talk to me except that it isn't exactly me she's talking to. She never speaks to me in English, only in French. I never hear her speak English. I carry her name as my second name, Mariette.

In one of the fading black and white photographs

I have of my grandmother, she stands in-between my grandfather and my father. While they look towards the person taking the photograph she looks somewhere else. Her head is turned as she focuses on something or someone on her left-hand side. The photograph must have been taken in South Africa or Kenya where they spent some time. I know this because she has draped a cardigan over her shoulders. She wears a pearl necklace and pearl earrings. The photograph is a tiny square and its left-hand corner has a crease. I keep the photograph in a frame with a postcard written to my grandmother with New Year's wishes for 1927. The postcard is addressed to *M'elle Mariette Laporte, Anse Royale*. It is signed by someone called Felise Benoiton and while the ink is fading I make out the words *Le parfum des fleurs ... éternel.*

In some ways, my parents are a map to who it is I am and where it is I come from. In other ways they are not. English is my first language, but it is not theirs. Sometimes I pronounce words in the way that they would. Subtle shifts of stress and intonation. Then they speak through me. They make their presence known. I say the words 'tortoise' and 'melancholy' out loud. As I say them I hear myself mispronounce them. *Tort-oyze. Me-lan-koli.* At the boarding school in Johannesburg, I once said the word 'tortoise'. The girl sitting next to me said: 'Sounds like a speech defect to me.'

When my South African grandmother was alive, she told me stories about when she was young as we drank tea and ate rusks, at her flat in Hillbrow, Johannesburg. Hillbrow was dense and built up and everyone lived in flats. It was considered cosmopolitan. I think cosmopolitan meant whites from different European countries coming together to drink coffee. I mean proper coffee. Not the kind spooned out of a tin into a mug of hot water, milk and sugar. My grandmother told me that when she was at school her English teacher made her wear donkey's ears every time she spoke Afrikaans. I never asked her what form the ears took or how they were attached to her head. When I think of this story I imagine my grandmother as a little girl in a fairy tale with the ears of an actual donkey attached to her head. Many years after my grandmother's death in Johannesburg in the 1990s, I read a book by the Kenyan writer and intellectual Ngũgĩ wa Thiong'o and came across the image of the donkey once again. *'In Kenya English became more than a language: it was the language, and all the others had to bow before it in deference. Thus one of the most humiliating experiences was to be caught speaking Gĩkũyũ in the vicinity of the school. The culprit was given corporal punishment – three to five strokes of the cane on bare buttocks – or was made to carry a metal plate around the neck with inscriptions such as I AM STUPID or I AM A DONKEY.'*

My grandmother grew up on a farm in the Northern

Cape. She considered herself a city girl and modelled her wardrobe and strawberry blonde hair on the actresses in Hollywood films. When she was young, she played the piano accordion at parties. My grandfather left her for another woman. On Sundays she would make a pot roast with beef which she would stuff with cloves. The scent of cloves filled her flat and when we finished the roast she would dish up tinned peaches with custard. My grandmother would always insist on serving men before women. This made me angry. I didn't know how to make sense of the anger that would well up inside of me and sit in my throat.

My father brought my family to the island from Johannesburg in 1974. The Seychelles were still a British colony and the airport, which had only recently been built, had been opened on 20 March 1972 by Queen Elizabeth II. When we arrived we lived with Tante Hoppy. My mother tells me how she would find me talking to something in the room where we slept. She said that my eyes were focused on a thing she couldn't see. Later, we moved to another house. It had wooden floors that smelt of polish, and Boney M was always on the radio. One night I was woken up by someone talking. The person talking was not actually alive. He was the ghost of someone who used to live in the house before. He had a beard and he was sitting in a chair hovering just below the ceiling and talking to me or talking to himself. The chair he was sitting in was not unlike the ones in

Tante Hoppy's sitting room. I jumped out of bed and ran to my parents' bedroom screaming. As I ran I heard him laugh. When we first got to the island, my mother would drape mosquito nets over our beds at night. Spiders would climb up the nets while we slept. After some time, the mosquito nets disappeared and we lived comfortably with the insects and the lizards that would watch us from walls and ceilings. One night, no longer sleeping inside the net, something fell from the ceiling and woke me up. I felt it wriggling around in my hair and it stung.

Later on Nan Nan Alda passed away and then Tante Hoppy passed away. After she died, I went back to the house with my father; he looked sad. I said something but he didn't reply. The chairs sat there circling the room just as they always had.

Mountain

I had thought about death before. Tante Hoppy had died. My father's parents had died. I had comforted myself with the thought that my parents would only die once they were very old. A handful of fathers or mothers of school friends had already died by then. There was cancer, suicide and a heart attack or two. The more I told myself that it would never happen to me the more I developed an uneasy feeling in the pit of my stomach. It hooked itself deep inside my body and stayed there as I began to have recurring dreams. These dreams were not quite like the other dreams I had. Everything in these dreams was illuminated by a light. The more I dreamt the more I understood that the light functioned as an emphasis. This is the only way that I can think of to describe the sensation of the dreams. *Pay attention to this because it is important.* When I awake I know deep inside my body that something is going to change. After my grandfather died and before I was told the news of his death, I dreamt that he was walking on a road that led to the sea at Anse Royale. The road is called Les Canelles. In the dream, my grandfather is illuminated by the light and he is smiling.

My brother pulled the ring off my father's finger and put it on his own. Soon after, the ring fell into the sea at Anse Royale. It was during the monsoon months and the sea was rough and murky. The wind blew and the beach was smothered with seaweed. My brother ran all the way home, up the mountain where we lived, shouting: 'Papa's ring fell into the sea!' An hour later it was found resting on a bed of sand, coral and seaweed. The ring, which is a signet ring, is so old that the initials inscribed onto it have worn away. The ring was given to my father by Tante Hoppy and in time, perhaps, the initials will disappear altogether. At the hospital, my brother sat through the night holding my father's hand. As he lay dying, his breath barely entered his body and barely left. The night before, when no one was there, I went into his room and whispered into his ear. 'I love you.' There was nothing else to say. He moved his head slightly. I knew that he had heard me. After the last rites were said, my mother and I fell asleep on the cool concrete floor by the bed. We no longer hoped or thought. We just waited silently. It was going to happen. He was going to die. I heard church bells ringing as I slept. On the mountain, I would hear bells from the Catholic church, which was built by the sea below. The bells would announce every ritual and rite of passage. I hear my brother say: 'He's going.' Sunday morning, 11 July 1993.

In the minutes after my father's passing, a doctor who was on night duty came to make his death official. We watched her check his pulse and remove his oxygen mask. She didn't acknowledge us even though, in these minutes, we all stood around my father's bed and shared the same space. She smiled to herself as she removed the mask. I still wonder what it was she was smiling at. Between her and us was a vast and silent space. We were now on the other side. We would never hear his voice again. Before we left the hospital, I lifted the white sheet from my father's face. *One last look. Close to him one more time. This will be the last time I see him in the flesh.* But a body is not the same dead. It is a presence, but it is not fully there. When we are truly alive we are as much spirit as we are biological matter. *Isn't it this spirit that produces the sensation of true presence?* After my father died, I buried the memory of his presence. I buried this memory because I feared the kind of presence that exists in relation to absence. I feared ghosts and being haunted. In the days after my father died, my mother told me that he visited her at night and that she could feel him asleep next to her in bed. She could feel his presence. She could hear his voice. She heard him speak to her in French.

I didn't understand then that haunting is not necessarily about the ghosts that take on frightening forms in-between the worlds of the living and the dead. Haunting is also about the unbearable loss of someone you love. You try to bury the memory but then it makes its presence known obliquely, in ways that might surprise you. *Why did you do that? Why did you say that? Why did you make that choice?* You try to forget but there is no forgetting without remembering. This is the paradox of loss. This is what it means to be haunted. The human condition, in the most ordinary of senses, is a condition of haunting.

I am reading a letter from my father. It's dated 22 February 1989 and it was posted to me while I was at boarding school in South Africa. My father tells me about a garden he is planting with my sister. She was born in 1981, just over a decade after me. *Finally, after much discussion Tata's garden has commenced with voluminous instructions about her flowers, I told her and promised Her Highness my best and only my best.* And then he tells me about a poem he wants to write. *I'll get around to finishing your poem – it's all in my head. I have to put it on paper. It will come again soon. Saying good-bye and now write soon and see you soon.*

My mother drives us home after my father's death. We sit in the car in silence. The sun has just begun to rise and the sea on the left-hand side of the long narrow road is tinted pale pink. On the right hand side of the road, the land extends upwards towards mountainous terrain. Occasionally, through the dark green vegetation, granite rocks are visible, sometimes they are on the side of the sea and at other times they are on the side of the mountain. The road is empty and silent except for birdsong, which builds in intensity and then wanes as the light becomes brighter and the day becomes hotter.

Our home on the mountain was designed by my mother together with an architect who came from England to live on the island. The house was built high up amongst granite rocks, which she imagined as sculptural forms and walls. It is an A-frame and has many levels that stretch high up into the apex of the roof. It's not in the colonial style except that it has a verandah, which is raised high above the ground and looks out towards the garden, the coconut trees and the ocean. Pink bougainvillea winds itself in and out of the balustrade that runs across the edge of the verandah. Beneath, a flower bed is filled with shrubs and one or two frangipani trees. The frangipani flowers, white with lemon-coloured centres, emit sweet perfume. In a few years the house will be sold. In a few months, I will leave the house and never return except for one attempt to confront the past.

The house is becoming a ruin. I kneel down on the grass at the edge of what used to be the garden. My eyes begin to burn and then my knees start to itch. I look up at the house and see a child a short distance away. She is looking at me. She stands there still and silent. She looks at me intently and then she disappears. She is the only person I see at the house. It is late in the afternoon and silent. I get up from the grass and walk up to the verandah. The sliding doors that once separated the verandah from the inside of the house are no longer there. I go inside. There is nothing left except for a painting of a landscape of a waterfall somewhere on the island. The painting, which is monumental in scale, is suspended on a high wall. My mother commissioned the painting in the 1970s when the house was built. It is the only domestic object left.

I dream that I am walking along a road called Sweet-Escott. The entrance to the road that leads up to the house on the mountain is on Sweet-Escott. In my dream I see myself picking white flowers. The flowers, which are lilies, grow in marshy soil next to the graveyard at one end of Sweet-Escott and the other end leads to Les Canelles, the road my grandfather walked down in my dream. I lay the lilies on my father's grave. He is buried in the graveyard together with my grandmother and grandfather. Tante Hoppy is also buried there along with the ancestors I never met but only heard about.

Sweet-Escott road is named after a former British colonial administrator to the islands. The names of roads and places tell their own history. They offer up a palimpsest of the past and of other kinds of haunting. They tell stories about hierarchies and who was important enough to have something named after them and who was not. The road up the mountain is steep and hard to walk up. I would always zigzag from one side of the road to the other until I reached the top. I would pause to pick cinnamon leaves, which I crushed in my palm so I could inhale their scent.

All of the Creole men and women who worked on the plantation lived further up the mountain and I couldn't see their homes from mine. They called me *Mam'selle*. If we passed each other we would say *Bonswa* and that would be all.

On the mountain, cinnamon would be barked and laid out to dry, branches of bananas cut and hung in the pantry would ripen and all day long I would eat these bananas, small and sweet. Through the processes of colonial settlement and slavery, fruit trees were brought to the islands from other colonised regions around the world. This is why I grew up on fruits such as bananas, pineapples, mangoes and custard apples (which we called *zat*, the Creole name). Plantain would be cooked in coconut milk and sugar to make a dessert called *Ladob Banan* or sliced and fried to make chips. Outside the kitchen, there was a tamarind tree. I would break the shell in my hands and eat the seeded, sour flesh with sugar. Every night, dinner would be cooked by Evangeline, who also lived in the house and did all the cooking and cleaning. When I was a child, I would sit in the kitchen with Evangeline at night while she cooked and listened to the radio. She would stay with us during the week and travel back home on the weekends. She would tell me stories about getting all dressed up and going to the disco in Victoria. On one of my birthdays, she gave me a Ladybird book as a gift. She slept in a room at the top of the house and after work she didn't enter the spaces that, during the day, she would clean. She spoke to me in English.

There were many ways in which delineated social groups might come together on the island, but this coming together was always encircled by a relationship to power structures that are simultaneously historical and alive to the present. This is a social space where the idea of 'we' or 'us' or 'them' is neither innocent nor neutral. To mark up a world in these terms is to establish and perpetuate the existence of hierarchies.

Dengue fever is spread by mosquitoes and I had it more than once. My head would hurt and I would become delirious. An elderly Creole woman who knew the medicinal properties of plants would be called to the house to suggest treatment. Her name was Loi. Once, when we were children, Loi took my brother and me for a walk. We walked for a whole day through cinnamon bushes and coconut trees. We saw clove trees and smelt the scent of the cloves in the cool, damp air of the forest. Every so often, we would stop at clearings where wooden, thatched houses were situated. *The scent of smoke. Burning coconut husks.* Before we approached a house Loi would shout: 'Bonswa!' It was to let everyone know we were passing by. When I was about thirteen and I got sunstroke my father called on Loi. She and I sat on the verandah opposite each other. She put a segment of a citrus fruit in her mouth and chewed it while she looked at me. After taking it out of her mouth she stuck it on my forehead. It was sticky and wet and I felt silly sitting there with a piece of chewed citrus fruit on my forehead. I leant forward so that it would drop off.

On 29 June 1976 the Seychelles attained official independence from Britain and joined the Commonwealth of Nations. A coalition government was formed with James Mancham as president and France-Albert René as prime minister. The coalition was constituted by the Democratic Party (DP) and the Seychelles United Party (SPUP). On 4 and 5 June 1977, while Mancham was in London for the Queen's Silver Jubilee and the Commonwealth Summit, a coup d'état, led by René and the SPUP, took place. René formally became president on 5 June 1977. The SPUP was renamed the Seychelles People's Progressive Front (SPPF) and then in 2009 it became the People's Party or *Parti Lepep*. In 1979 the Seychelles was declared a one-party socialist state with the SPPF as the only legal party. In 1992, René was to announce a return to a multi-party system of governance.

In 1979, I was eight years old and understood the events of 1977–1979 through their relationship to my schooling. The state abolished private education and my mother told my brother and me that things had changed and we would have to leave the International School, which we had attended up until then. The school was now reserved solely for the children of non-Seychellois parents. The state put a new educational programme in place. It was called the National Youth Service or the NYS. My mother, opposed to the way in which political ideology and paramilitary training were incorporated into the school curriculum, decided to teach us herself. Every day my brother and I sat opposite each other at the dining room table while we worked through the schoolbooks my mother bought in Johannesburg. In the afternoons we would dive for shells in the bay at Anse Royale. In 1984, when I was thirteen years old, I was sent to boarding school in Johannesburg.

Another way in which I understood the coup was in relation to land that the state might confiscate. My parents were locked into an ideological battle between the social, economic and political principles of socialism and those of capitalism. My mother wanted to leave the island but my father wanted to stay. Sometimes, in the middle of the night, crockery would fly around the house and I would hear my parents shouting. My father couldn't let go of the land and when he asked me if I wanted to leave the island. I shook my head and said no and this 'no' was without ambiguity. From childhood, I was conscious of an emotional bond to my home on the mountain and the land that surrounded it and, as I grew older, I was conscious of not wanting to give it up. Now I can see that my identity and sense of self were wound up in my father's name and in the possession of this land. It was only later that I came to fully grasp and develop a language for what was truly at stake and for whom. I would come to see how I was positioned within a history embedded in racial violence and white entitlement. I came to see this because of how I experienced South Africa and the logic of white supremacy. I came to see the human capacity for brutality and the many ways in which it could materialise, ways that were not necessarily always that obvious. I saw myself in this history.

Around the time of my father's death, I found a volume of poetry published by Hazel de Silva. Her mother was Seychelloise and her father was Sri-Lankan. She was born in Nairobi, Kenya in 1947 and she died in 1996. The book of poems, titled *Sega of Seychelles*, was published in 1983. Sega is the name of a dance that by the time I was a child in the 1970s was very popular on the islands and was danced by everyone. It was also part of the entertainment put on for tourists. But cultural forms such as Sega also emerged from the experience of slavery and were mediums through which social and political commentary could be made.

Here in Mahé
day after day
the sun shines
with a burning heat
so fierce

the worker
on coco plantation
or cinnamon
is falling with the chaleur

with an empty future
the islander
appears like a ghost
out of the mountain
morning mists

On the island, I listened to the conversations of grown-ups. I listened to stories about people who disappeared. The grown-ups would often mention a man called Gérard Hoarau who was exiled to London where he was assassinated. This was in 1985 when I was fourteen years old. He was shot on the doorstep of his home. In 1992 my father was arrested and put in jail for four days. They said he was plotting a coup d'état. During the 1980s, when my brother and I would arrive at Mahé airport from boarding school in Johannesburg, airport security would confiscate our cassettes for a day or two. Security officials would listen to them for any messages. They thought that my father was involved in a plan to overthrow

René and that we were helping our father smuggle messages from South Africa.

In 2018, when I am forty-seven years old, I start reading a book called *The Seychelles Islands and its First Landowners 1786–1833*. It's by Julien Durup, a Seychellois archivist and historian, and it was published in 2013. '*At the beginning of 1830, slaves who were registered in the Seychelles mostly originated from Mozambique, Madagascar, India, Malaysia, Santo Domingo and various undocumented places.*' For the first time, I read about a slave who is named as Pompee and I read a story of resistance and burning. '*In one case, on 9th July 1810, Pompee a slave was burnt alive (as retribution for killing his estate manager), by the authorisation of Jean-Baptise Queau-Quinssy the French commandant of Seychelles. According to history Queau-Quissy was not a reputable person, he stole the land allocated to future priests, and was involved in corruption ... In spite of all that, he has been immortalised twice after our independence. A statue of him was erected in the State House garden, and the new Foreign Affairs' building was also named after him ... Nothing was done up to now to commemorate the burning alive of Pompee our famous hero. Maroons were very common and slaves in transit revolted on many occasions. In 1786, they burnt 'l'ile Longue' which was a slave depot used mostly by the Portuguese to recuperate and disorientate the slaves. The next year they also burnt Cerf Island to the ground, and they burnt it again later in 1832. The effects of the blaze on the hilly part on the two islands are still visible.'*

A military truck filled with soldiers in camouflage raced up the mountain. It was late in the afternoon and soon the sun would go down. I was sitting with my mother, my brother and my baby sister outside in the garden. I was eleven or twelve years old. We were waiting for my father to come home from work. The soldiers brought the truck to a halt and jumped out with AK-47s. We watched them run into the house and fan out up the mountain. Then they jumped back into the truck and drove off as quickly as they had arrived. *Don't move. Just sit still.* I don't know what I thought or felt. Soon afterwards my father came home from work and it was obvious that he had been punched in the face. I knew, even though I was still young and just emerging from childhood, that this event had something to do with my father's opinions about the one-party state. But I didn't really know, with any precision, why the soldiers had visited us that afternoon. Now when I think of their visit, it is bathed in grey-green light. I see the green of the grass underneath my bare feet, the shadowy forms of my mother, my brother and my sister next to me, the dogs that lay around us, the soldiers fanning out ... I hear my mother's voice ... I see my father's ashen face as he returns home. That night we slept on lumpy mattresses, between chairs, on the floor in Tante Hoppy's sitting room.

In 1994, when I was twenty-three years old, I slept for the last time in my bedroom in the house on the mountain. After the deaths of both my grandparents, I inherited their bed. The bed was large and Edwardian and it was painted white with brass decorations that had loosened and rattled when I moved. In front of the bed was a rocking chair that had belonged to my grandmother. The rocking chair had decorative bent wood rockers and a rattan seat and back. In this chair, I had dreamt of what my life could be and in-between dreaming I read books: *Anna Karenina*, *Madame Bovary*, *Tess of the D'Urbervilles*. These books made me feel depressed because all the women who made choices for themselves ended up dying or unhappy.

I read *Wide Sargasso Sea*. Its author, Jean Rhys, also grew up on an island and this is the first compelling fact about her life. Her father was a Welsh doctor and her mother was a white West Indian. Charlotte Brontë's Mrs Rochester becomes Rhys's Creole heiress Antoinette Cosway. Rhys gave Austen's feral attic-inhabiting arsonist feelings, thoughts, opinions, desires and a history. *She gave her a voice.* I have never encountered a female character in a book that might give form and substance to my memories and my experience of the world. Sometimes, I see glimpses of myself in characters but they belong to other times and other places. There is always something missing. In Rhys's *Smile Please: An Unfinished Autobiography*, she describes a frangipani tree and then a hibiscus flower. Her words connect me to her: '*I was wearing the new white dress, a birthday present, and a wreath of frangipani. A frangipani tree grew not far from the house; it was sometimes bare, even of leaves, then suddenly covered with pink sweet-smelling flowers. If you broke a branch it bled copiously, not red blood but white. Hibiscus, at least the hibiscus I know, fades soon after it is picked, but frangipani flowers last and are very easy to make into wreaths.*'

When we lived on the mountain, I was not allowed to go anywhere or speak to anyone on my own. From the verandah of our house, I could see the sea and the horizon. Once or twice I rebelled and walked to the beach on my own. The men that passed me in the road hissed and whistled. On the beach opposite Tante Hoppy's house, I saw a white Italian man with a Creole girl who was then around my own age, perhaps twelve or thirteen. I watched him with her in the sea and what I saw made me uneasy. He was much older than her and I remember that he had a beard and a large, white belly. I listen to grown-ups tell stories about men and young girls. Some of the men were Europeans who came to live or holiday on the island. Others were Seychellois men. There were stories about how a girl was raped in the graveyard. My mother was consumed by fear. My father had a friend who held me too tightly every time he said hello or goodbye. It made my hackles rise. It made me angry but I never said anything. One day, following an argument with my mother I stormed off down the mountain. An elderly Creole woman in a hat and a long floral skirt like the ones Nan Nan Alda wore stopped me and asked me why I was walking alone. A few minutes later, my mother drove up behind me in her car. I felt relieved because even as I rebelled I was afraid. I was afraid of walking alone. *My heart would beat faster and my palms would sweat.*

In the middle of the night, after everyone went to sleep, I would walk downstairs to the verandah to look up at the sky and the stars. I looked for each of the constellations, which glittered in my imagination and filled the sky with a vividness I have never seen again. Sometimes, I walked off the verandah onto the lawn. I would never walk to the bottom of the lawn and would always stay close to the verandah's edge. If it was full moon the white frangipani flowers, which had fallen from the trees onto the grass, would gleam in the semi-darkness. I would pick one and inhale its scent. Then I would read into the night. As I read, dogs barked across the mountain. At sunrise, cockerels would crow and frogs would chatter by the dam below the slope of coconut trees outside my bedroom window. After sunrise, I would lie in bed and listen for my parents in the kitchen, which was below my bedroom. I would nestle deeper into my bed and listen to the hum of their conversations.

River

In the spring, the jacarandas trees are dense with purple flowers, which thickly carpet the surfaces onto which they fall. *If one of the flowers drops on your head you will have good luck.* If you have ever lived in Johannesburg, the trees will be embedded in your memory. Jacarandas are not indigenous to South Africa and it is thought that they were brought in from Argentina in the late nineteenth century.

We sit under the jacaranda trees as we drink tea and eat sandwiches that are cut into triangles and stacked up on stainless steel platters. In the afternoon, we sit again underneath the trees and drink tea and eat cake. Dave brings the sandwiches, the cake and the tea. He wears a white uniform. Dave is not his real name. But we are told to call him Dave. There is a space between him and us. No one tries to enter this space and no one mentions it.

Behind the jacaranda trees there are stone steps that lead down to a rose garden and a sundial. We hardly ever walk there. We are to walk where the teachers can see us. There are rules. What is and what isn't allowed is palpable. After we finish afternoon tea, we return to our dormitories, walking up towards a large white building that was once a family home. It has a deep, cool veranda, a red tiled roof and tall gables in the Cape Dutch style. The whiteness of the building reverberates against the blueness of the sky and the intensity of the light.

Sir Herbert Baker designed the building, which was once called Bedford Court, for the mining magnate Sir George Farrar. Mining magnates are also referred to as Randlords after the Witwatersrand – 'Rand' – in what was then the Transvaal province. In 1892, Baker left England for Cape Town and it was there that he was to secure the patronage of Cecil John Rhodes who, between 1890 and 1896, was Prime Minister of the Cape. Buildings, like the one occupied by my school, exist because of the story of mining in South Africa. They are the material manifestations of social aspiration and its historical relationship to white power. George Farrar settled in Johannesburg soon after the discovery of gold and he lived at Bedford Court with his wife Lady Ella Farrar and their six daughters.

Following the official transition from apartheid to democracy in 1994, part of the Transvaal, including the Witwatersrand, was incorporated into the newly formed Gauteng province, which means 'Place of Gold' in the Sotho languages. You can still see the mine dumps left by the gold rush of 1886. I used to think that the mine dumps were beautiful, aglow at sunset. But now all I see are tombs. The wind blows the dust from the dumps into the gardens and homes of the people that live in proximity to them. The dust, which is laced with toxic substances such as uranium, gets into their lungs. Underneath Johannesburg acidic water is rising in abandoned mine shafts, leaching into the groundwater and flowing into rivers.

In 1920, Bedford Court was bought by Jean Fletcher who, together with Jessie Johnston, had founded the St Andrews School for girls in Johannesburg in 1902. By 1920, as the school expanded, it needed new premises. Both the founders of the school were Scottish and the St Andrews flag would fly on a flag pole located on an emerald green lawn. Unless there were special circumstances, you were only allowed to walk on the lawn in your final year at the school. If you stepped onto it without permission you would receive some form of reprimand or punishment. Flower beds bordered the lawn and steps led up to a portico with white columns where, on spring evenings, I could smell the sweet scent of jasmine flowers. Across from the St Andrews flag, a small pavilion had benches where private conversations might be had. Nearby, steps led up to the front doors of the library in which I would find novels to read. In this library, I found books about dystopian worlds. I read George Orwell's *1984* and William Golding's *Lord of the Flies*. Later, at university in Johannesburg, I would connect these stories to Margaret Atwood's *The Handmaid's Tale*. They gave me a *language* for mechanisms of dehumanisation and scapegoating to which I began to bear witness.

When I first arrived at the school in 1984, I began in the junior school which was located away from the senior school. It had its own library, and one day, the girls with whom I shared a dormitory locked me in. They had stolen the keys from the man who cleaned it at the end of the day. They locked me in after saying things. I don't recall exactly what they said but I do remember how their words made me feel. The man who cleaned the library told them to leave me alone. They paid him no attention. One night, after the episode in the library, I punched one of the girls in the face. She was the ringleader of the gang that had locked me up. She had green eyes and short curly dark blonde hair. I punched her after the gang circled my bed after lights out. The next day, I was called into the headmistress's office and told off. The girl's lip had swelled up and cracked. Some of the girls in my class came up to me to ask me how it was I could have done such a thing. This was the first time some of them had ever spoken to me.

A long driveway takes you to the official entrance of the senior school. As you travel down the driveway, you have time to contemplate the importance of what is in front of you and your access to it. You have time to feel the sensations of belonging or not belonging. In the white world, power is constellated around two specific language groups, English and Afrikaans. The world of St Andrews is English-speaking, not only in a linguistic sense, but also in the sense of its cultural and social codes, which function in relation to economic and societal aspirations. It is through empire that particular kinds of class anxieties travelled downwards from the northern to the southern hemisphere where they came to lodge themselves in the psychological and emotional life of the settlers and their descendants. At the school you were to learn the English-speaking world through atmospheres, through pressures.

Atmospheres, feelings and sensations teach me about other kinds of truth; not the kind of truth that claims objectivity and detachment. In attending the school that was once Bedford Court, the Farrar homestead, I begin to learn about educational spaces that were founded on the belief in the supremacy of the white race. I begin to understand who is close to economic capital and thus to power. I learn about desires that germinated in the northern hemisphere, travelling south towards the Cape and then north again towards Johannesburg. In these buildings I come to know the biographies of the men who brought particular kinds

49

of architecture and spatial arrangements into being. I can trace violence. I can trace many different kinds of violence including the violence of racism and xenophobia and the resistance to it. Some of this violence remains unwritten and unspoken. Some of it is overt and some of it is subtle.

One evening, in the wood-panelled dining room, an English teacher supervising us as we ate overheard me say the word 'here'. I can't remember the sentence into which this 'here' was inserted. Suddenly, as if from nowhere, the teacher stopped my conversation and said: 'No. It is pronounced "here" [extended, open vowel sound] not "here" [short, flat vowel].' I looked up at her in surprise. She sounded irritated and her irritation made me feel that I had done something terribly wrong. Except that I didn't know what it was. I learnt that my 'here' was said with a flattened vowel sound and that I was supposed to open my mouth wider. I was supposed to open it wider in order to stretch out the sound.

Desmond Tutu, who was by then a bishop and a Nobel Peace Prize laureate, once led a Saturday morning chapel service at the school. The school, which was private and hence governed by a separate examination board, allowed in girls that were not white although, at the time, this was only a small minority. In this way, within the context of the apartheid state, the school had liberal inclinations. But these kinds of inclinations were already always complicit in forms of violence that were not necessarily visible or audible. Of course, the relationship to visibility and invisibility, to audibility and inaudibility, depended on what it was you were able to see and hear. It was also dependent on how you looked and how you listened. You might see what I mean or you might not. It is still very difficult to explain the covert ways in which cultures of white dominance operate. Sometimes, these cultures appear to be magnanimous. But if you are somehow on a margin or even outside of it you might become familiar with the limitations of this magnanimity. You might begin to see where magnanimity fails and the points at which it collapses into prejudice, xenophobia and racism.

Sometimes the thoughts and feelings accumulated over centuries spill out in slips of the tongue and in the almost indiscernible gestures of condescension. Sometimes you are taken by surprise. You think that you are part of something until you realise that you are not. There are many ways to imagine a border and there can be a certain banality to how a border is policed.

It's 1991 and I'm twenty years old. I'm sitting next to my boyfriend in the university canteen just before dinner. His parents are sitting opposite us. Unlike my parents his parents are English-speaking. Through the windows the Johannesburg sky is orange. I'm sitting at the table but somehow I'm also floating above it. The room starts to feel like a gigantic spaceship hovering in the sky. I feel my back pressing against the chair. I feel a knot between my shoulder blades. I look down at the surface of the canteen table, which has a wooden veneer. Someone had spilt some coffee, which is now cold and grey. There are sprinkles of sugar in the little puddle of coffee and on the surface around it. I press a finger down onto the sugar and it sticks. I rub the sugar off with the paper serviette scrunched in my other hand. In this space and time I am a presence. Yet, somehow, I am also an absence. I am negative space. *I must be imagining things. I'm sure they've seen me.* I wait for his parents to look at me. I wait for them to ask me something. But they don't. They only look at him. I feel shame. But I don't understand why it is I should feel this shame. I look at his mother out of the corner of my eye. If you happened to meet her you might think. *Look at how beautiful she is. Look at how well-dressed she is. She's so well-spoken, so refined, so charming.* I want to get up and leave but I can't. I want to walk away but I'm somehow glued to the chair that I'm sitting on. Afterwards, he says: 'Oh, when they looked at you they thought you were Indian.' He adds: 'They're taking us out for dinner.' I don't know why I agree to go to dinner with them, but I do. At the restaurant, his parents shake my hand. They smile at me. They order a bottle of wine. 'We see now. You are French. That is what you are.'

As an undergraduate, English literature was one

of my majors. We studied Chaucer, Shakespeare, Austen, Dickens, the Romantic poets and other things related to England, a place I had never visited but that had been imprinted on my cultural and historical imagination. I signed up for an optional module called African and Caribbean Literature. One of the books was *Maru* by Bessie Head, who was an anti-apartheid activist as well as a journalist, teacher and writer. In 1964 she was exiled to Botswana. *'Bessie Head was the daughter of a white woman and black man. After her mother's parents found she was pregnant she was sent to a mental asylum, where Head was born on 6 July 1937.'* Maru was written in 1971. My edition was published in 1987 and reprinted in 1988 and 1989. Near the beginning of the book, I had underlined the adjective *different* and written the noun *difference* in the margin. *'The white man found only too many people who looked <u>different</u> ... That was all that outraged the receivers of his discrimination ... And if the white man thought that Asians were a low, filthy nation, Asians could still smile with relief – at least, they were not Africans. And if the white man thought Africans were a low, filthy nation, Africans in Southern Africa could still smile – at least they were not Bushmen. They all have their monsters. You just have to look different from them, the way the facial features of a Sudra or Tamil do not represent the features of a high caste Hindu, then seemingly anything can be said and done to you as your outer appearance reduces you to the status of a non-human being.'*

The text of a play is imprinted on my memory. Its title is *WOZA ALBERT!* by Percy Mtwa, Mbongeni Ngema and Barney Simon. I had drawn attention to important lines in pencil but the marks made by my pencil are fading and the pages are yellowing. Near the beginning, the characters talk about the passbook that controlled movement along racial lines. The dialogue is short and snappy; the words do not hide their meaning. They say things as they are. I read the words out loud. I am in my body but at the same time I am in the body of another. There is a voice inside my head:

You are prohibited. You are prohibited to move from where we have placed you without this pass. This is inscribed in law. You do not have the rights of an adult. Your skin colour signifies all manner of things. The darker it is the further away from us you are. You are not allowed to do as you please. We will let you know when you may inhabit our spaces, our streets, our pavements, our properties. Don't sit on the same benches as us. Don't get too close. We'll decide when you are allowed in and when you must leave. You are forbidden from speaking back. You are forbidden from speaking out. Some of us might invite you in. Some of us might even smile at you and offer you a cup of tea. But know this. You are not equal to us. If one of us decides to love you we will make life a misery. We will make it a living hell. We will haunt you. We will haunt you until your dying day...

We are different. We're not bad people. We might not be perfect but then who is? At a family dining room table on Sunday afternoon in Johannesburg as the last dregs of red wine linger at the bottom of the cut crystal glasses I hear one of the men tell a racist joke. The words are without ambiguity. There is also something about the way in which the words are uttered. I hear laughter. I look up. One of the men is not laughing. He talks back to them. He says something to them about what it is they have said. *Snap back. Snap back and see what happens.* They laugh at him and then they humiliate him with words coated in laughter. He gets up from the table. Now, he is silent. His face is pale. I look down at my plate. The plate is white. In front of the plate on the tablecloth, which is white, there is a stain. Someone poured me a glass of red wine and some of it trickled down the wrong side of the glass all the way down to the tablecloth. There is a lull. For a moment, it's quiet. I hear someone at the table shift in their chair. I stand up to take some plates back to the kitchen. 'Here you go Slave Girl', one of the women says, handing me her empty plate and then she laughs.

In the 1990s, the mythical ideal of a Rainbow Nation took hold in the South African imagination. The image of the rainbow managed to elide centuries of colour-coded violence. I was swept up in national euphoria. The Rainbow Nation was the subject of much debate. South African scholars and intellectuals drew attention to the glibness of its promise. The

South African scholar and intellectual Pumla Gqola wrote about the ways in which *'rainbowism was evoked at specific points where a certain kind of non-racialism, though not necessarily anti-racism, needs to be stressed. We are not always rainbow people, only some of the time when the need arises.'*

After they had killed him, by shooting him on the top of the head with a Makarov pistol, they had a *braai* (a barbecue) and drank while they waited for his body to burn on a pyre of tyres and wood. His name was Sizwe Kondile and he was a student activist murdered in 1981 by apartheid operatives aligned to the covert police unit called Vlakplaas. At the South African Truth and Reconciliation Commission, broadcast nationally by South African radio and television media between 1996 and 2001, one of Kondile's murderers, the former Vlakplaas Captain Dirk Coetzee, said that he would like to meet Kondile's mother and look her in the eye. In his testimony, Coetzee had emphasised that the burning of a body to ashes takes about seven hours. While Kondile's body burnt they had to pass the time. This is why they decided to have a *braai* and drink. Kondile's mother, Charity Nongqalelo Kondile, sent this message via her counsel Adu Imran Moosa: 'Mrs Kondile asks me to convey to you that [meeting you] is an honour that she feels you do not deserve and that if you were really remorseful you would not have applied for amnesty but in fact stood trial for what you did with her son.'

I'm sitting in a university seminar in Johannesburg with other students and a few academics and professors. We're part of a research group. I'm thirty-four years old. 2005. We're sitting around a table. The table has a kind of mythical presence that is not easily forgotten. It's monumental and constructed out of solid wood. The wood is rough-hewn and has uneven surfaces and edges. It's as if the table is attempting to perform a certain kind of gravitas. From the table, a white professor utters: 'Race is no longer an issue in South Africa.' I look across at her. For a moment the room is silent. A black academic says: 'Race is very much an issue in South Africa.' The voices are on different sides of the table. The voices have colours, they have textures, they have genders, they have history and they have particular relationships to power. Not long after this, the black academic disappears. His disappearance is mentioned only in passing. A few years later, one of the students from the research group tells me that the black academic is living on the streets, somewhere in Johannesburg. The student, who is now a professional academic, says: 'You know, he was never right in the head.' I wonder if he really believes this or if it's just easier to go along with the institutional narrative. Then, he tells me that a group of white academics wrote to the white professor and told her that she'd better find a way to get rid of him. He said things they didn't like. One day, the white professor named me Island Girl and sent me off to buy her sandwiches at lunchtime. I told her how this made me feel. *After all, this is a*

*university. I'm no longer a girl. I'm now well into
my thirties. You must understand what it means to
juxtapose the words 'island' and 'girl'. You must
understand. You must see.* Then she said something
about my state of mind.

'Why do you use these words "black" and "white"?'
This question was asked in another time and place;
far away from the life I lived in Johannesburg. It
was directed at me by a professor at a university in
London in 2015. Forty-four years old. *I'm stuck in
language. I'm stuck in my history and I'm consumed
by anger. This anger has taken up residence in my
body.* Perhaps the professor was trying to say that
I am supposed to be thinking about how the world
could be. *I was not supposed to be seeing race.* A
year or two before another professor had said to
me: 'We know all that. No need to repeat what we
already know. Say something new.' I wanted to say
that I didn't put that much weight on newness and
academic fashions but I bit my tongue. I tried to
find a way to tell the professor that we don't know
anything and that we weren't even reading what
black scholars writing about racism had already
theorised. I wanted to ask her who she included in
the 'we' of 'we know all that'. *But the words stuck
in my throat.* Only recently a white academic from
South Africa had asked me where the black scholars
were because she had never heard of them. Academic
citation practices, in the worlds within which I
move, are embedded in ideas about who is important

enough to be seen, who is important enough to speak and who is important enough to be heard. I wanted to highlight the fact that I was a white scholar talking about black people's experience of racism; that I wasn't a detached, impartial observer. I wanted to talk about complicity. Any violence I might have experienced doesn't negate my own capacity for violence. I wanted to talk about absence and silence and the things I couldn't yet see. *I wanted to talk about the struggle to find a language to express the things I was feeling. I wanted to say the unsayable.* In London, in this other time and place, much is made of freedom of speech. But when I say things that go against the grain of accepted thought the atmosphere bristles and almost indiscernible pressures nudge me further and further away from a circle I can feel rather than see.

White supremacy has had so many different manifestations in my life. When I say manifestations I am not only referring to things that are overt, the kinds of things that South African intellectuals refer to as the *spectacle of apartheid*. The South African scholar, writer and intellectual Njabulo Ndebele famously mobilised the idea of spectacle to critique the dramatisation of social relations, inter-racial encounters and narrative in black South African literature. I am also referring to things that are much more hidden, much more insidious. Sometimes these things are so deeply buried they have not yet entered into consciousness and inhabit worlds of feeling or the kind of knowledge that has yet to make its way into language. When I use words such as 'white' and 'black' I am not re-stating colonial and apartheid categories as if to fix them and impose a violence of my own. *How do you show colour-blindness? How do you perform it and why?*

I started reading Frantz Fanon's *Black Skin. White Masks* in Johannesburg in about 2005. The book was first published in French in 1952 and then in English in 1967. I started looking for books that could help me to give a shape to half-formed thoughts and emotions, for the things I had witnessed. *'I believe that the fact of the juxtaposition of the white and black races has created a massive psychoexistential complex. I hope by analysing it to destroy it. This book is a clinical study. Those who recognise themselves in it, I think, will have made a step forward … I move slowly in the world, accustomed now to seek no longer for upheaval. I progress by crawling. And already I am dissected by white eyes, the only real eyes. I am fixed. Having adjusted their microtomes, they objectively cut away slices of my reality. I am laid bare.'*

When I finish reading Frantz Fanon I started reading Steve Biko's writings published in a book titled I Write What I Like. It was first published in London in 1978 and then in South Africa in 1996 and my edition was published in Johannesburg in 2004. I learn about the philosophy underpinning the Black Consciousness movement in South Africa. *'So we argued that any changes which are to come can only come as a result of a programme worked out by black people ... for black people to work out a programme they needed to defeat the one main element in politics which was working against them: a psychological feeling of inferiority which was deliberately cultivated by the system. So equally, too, the whites in order to be able to listen to blacks needed to defeat the one problem which they had, which was one of 'superiority'.'*

I read about Steve Biko's death. *'On 18 August 1977, he was again detained under section 6 of the Terrorism Act. He was taken to Port Elizabeth, where he was kept naked and manacled, as was revealed at the inquest after his death. He died in detention on 12 September. The cause of death was established as brain damage.'*

Winnie Madikizela-Mandela's journal surfaced forty-one years after she was released from sixteen months in detention. These writings, written in secret, were first published in 2013. *'On a freezing-cold winter's morning some hours before dawn, on Monday 12 May 1969, security police arrived at the Soweto home of Winnie Mandela and detained her in the presence of her two young daughters.'* I stop at a passage in which Winnie Mandela describes her detention. I re-read this passage because it speaks about violence enacted by a white woman on a black woman. *'I am next to the assault chamber. As long as I live I shall never forget the nightmares I have suffered as a result of the daily prisoners' piercing screams as the brutal corporal punishment is inflicted on them, sometimes a hose pipe, you feel it tearing at your own flesh mercilessly. It's hard to imagine women inflicting so much punishment. I have shed tears time without number quite unconsciously and often forget even to wipe them off. These hysterical screams pierce through my heart and injure my dignity so much. The hero of these assaults is barely 23 years old, very often the screaming voice appealing for mercy is that of a mother twice her age but of course she is white, a matron [at] that, this qualifies her for everything. The prisoner is at her mercy, life and all. She even bangs their heads against my cell wall in her fury. As the blood spurts from the gaping wounds she hits harder.'*

My mother studied anatomy in apartheid South Africa. She tells me this story over and over again: *'We had to do a year of dissection. The corpses lay row upon row. They were covered with thick plastic on cement plinths in a huge hall. I was 17, almost 18. There were four students per corpse. Most of the bodies were of young black men. They told us that they were the bodies of men whose families had not claimed them. The professor would lift the plastic and introduce us. He would give the corpses names.'*

While at the boarding school, I sometimes spent weekends at the home of one of the girls. When her parents were out, Miriam, who was the maid, asked me if I could talk to her about something. In post-apartheid South Africa, women that were once referred to as maids are called domestic workers. But in the 1980s they were called maids. Miriam slept in a small room at the back of my friend's house. I knew that we were under a decade apart in age and that this generational proximity produced an intimacy. At the same time, each of us understood, although neither of us said anything, that this intimacy was already compromised. I sat down next to Miriam on her bed and she started to tell me that her brother has gone missing in Soweto. In the 1980s I associated Soweto with something called 'township unrest', which I only vaguely understood. Miriam was crying. She said: 'I don't know where my brother is. I think he has been killed. No one knows where he is.' As she spoke, I started crying too and then I couldn't stop. I don't know why I couldn't stop. The sadness engulfed us and drew us closer. My friend walked into the room and listened to the story. The next day, Miriam left and I never saw her again. Nobody said anything about her departure.

Soweto (South Western Townships) emerged in the 1930s from peri-urban locations that grew from mining. Through the first decades of the twentieth century urban life, and what could and couldn't be possible, was filtered through a racist lens. The Native Urban Areas Act (1923) attempted to segregate housing and curtail freedom of movement. After the

National Party won the election in 1948, apartheid, an ideological and bureaucratic system of complete racial segregation, could be fully realised. The Group Areas Act (1950) systematically segregated people into racially demarcated areas. Soweto was where people classified black were located. Throughout the twentieth century in South Africa, black people were labelled in various ways: Bantu, Natives, Blacks, Africans. Then, there was a category for those identified as Asians. The category Coloured included convoluted subclassifications subsumed under 'Mixed or other Coloured'. People from countries from Mauritius to Syria were included in this not-white-enough category.

In the 1990s, I travelled to a wedding reception in Soweto with some friends. As we entered Soweto, someone started laughing: 'All you whiteys in the car, are your hearts beating faster?' 'Yes', we laugh back, 'our hearts are beating faster.' We drove past matchbox houses, the kind of housing provided by the apartheid state. They were dubbed matchbox houses because of their scale.

My mother told me that after she became a physiotherapist in the 1960s she worked in Soweto at the Baragwanath Hospital, or 'Bara' as it is referred to in South Africa. It was by then an important teaching hospital linked to the University of the Witwatersrand in Johannesburg. Now the hospital is known as The Chris Hani Baragwanath Hospital after the leader of the South African Communist Party. Thembisile Chris Hani was assassinated on 10 April 1993 by Januzs Waluś, who had emigrated to South Africa from Poland in 1981. Waluś, who is anti-communist, had links to the Afrikaner Weerstandsbeweging (AWB), a white supremacist organisation in South Africa. Baragwanath was the surname of a Cornishman, John Albert. He had bought the land in the late nineteenth century and established a trading store, refreshment post and hotel. In the early 1940s the British government bought the land and built the Imperial Military Hospital for Commonwealth soldiers. Then between 1947 and 1948 it became a civilian hospital and patients were transferred there from what was called the non-European wing of the Johannesburg General Hospital. My mother has a photograph of herself with a patient in a ward at Baragwanath. The colours in the photograph have begun to wash out and now it has a purplish tinge.

In the privileged white English- and Afrikaans-speaking suburbs in which I moved, I heard pejorative names that were also anti-Semitic and xenophobic. Within this atmosphere, Greek and Portuguese immigrants were also in the firing line. Insults were honed on the school playground and English- and Afrikaans-speakers developed a lexicon of insults for each other. But there was no line between those who perpetrated violence and those who didn't. Every person in these white worlds was capable of it even though they themselves might have been a target of prejudice themselves. Prejudice in all its manifestations was so ordinary it wasn't necessarily noticed. It was in the air and in the atmosphere. Jokes and throwaway comments were laced with prejudice and every kind of racism. *It's only a joke. Where's your sense of humour? Smile. You should smile more. Show us some teeth.*

One day, many years after the official transition from apartheid and well into the new millennium, a black friend invited me to a party at her house. She introduced me to her friends. 'I didn't know you had white friends.' He said it sardonically and I laughed.

1984. A school trip is planned. A bus will take us from Johannesburg to the Eastern Transvaal, which has now been re-named Mpumalanga. On the bus, I stare out of the window at aloe plants growing on rocky hillsides by the road. Aloes are succulents with intense orange flowers. I take out a sketch book and I start to draw them. I draw their outlines and then I start to colour them in with orange pencils. The flowers make me think of fire. I am sitting somewhere near the front of the bus. The seats next to mine are empty. Groups of girls talk and laugh behind mine. As I am drawing, one of the girls comes up to me. She edges in close so that it feels as though her face is up against mine. One body enters the space of another without invitation or prior intimacy. I freeze. I don't say anything. I know that something is going to come out of her mouth and that it is going to feel bad. 'You have pig eyes. Your eyes are so small, just like pigs. Your nose is so big.'

The bus stops at a hotel in Pilgrim's Rest, one of the places where, in the 1870s, prospectors came looking for gold. Now it's a tourist destination and we get out of the bus and stand around as we wait for the teachers to tell us what to do next. It's late in the afternoon. There's a chill in the air and soon the sun will go down. I look across at one of the teachers. I see something in her face. I am not quite sure what it is I see but the air is heavy. I feel the unease. The teacher is talking to the only black girl in the class. In a few moments it will become clear that she is barred from staying at the hotel. She is barred because she is black. She has to stay somewhere else.

Somebody's money is stolen. A teacher decides that she will find the thief. There is no actual evidence. There is no way of knowing who took the money from the girl's locker. The teacher uses a system of detection that is already at play in the apartheid state at large. This is the 1980s and, in the areas designated non-white, wars are raging. The rule is that if anything is stolen it's the black person, although it must also be said that the word person is not often placed in proximity to the word black. The history teacher calls the accused to her classroom for a chat. Afterwards, I see the girl crying. She is the same girl who wasn't allowed to sleep in the hotel with the white girls. She is the same girl who was barred from the hotel on the school trip. One Monday morning, she arrived at the school shaken. She had been driven to school from Soweto where she lived with her parents. She had witnessed something on her way in. I asked her what she had seen and she told me. What she had seen was not spoken at the school and I have never told anyone.

Unearthed

I unpack. I put photographs of my parents, my grandparents and Tante Hoppy on a bookshelf next to my grandmother's crystal glasses. The glasses are all different shapes and sizes. They are fragile and they are variously engraved with abstract patterns or motifs like leaves, flowers or grapes. The glasses no longer sparkle. They sit on my shelf like artefacts from another time and place. After my father's death, I carried these glasses from Mahé Island to Johannesburg. Now, I have carried them to London. A photograph of Tante Hoppy and my grandmother standing on either side of my grandfather sits in the palm of my hand. It has a white border and its edges are deckled. They are standing on the beach at Anse Royale. I know this because of the inscription written in fading blue ink on the back. It includes a date: 23

February 1962. Tante Hoppy wears an elegant dress, a pearl necklace and a hat. My grandfather wears a suit and tie. My grandmother, Mariette, turns slightly towards him and loops her arm around his. They are all smiling.

Daydreaming. Mahé Island, Seychelles, it's the 1970s and I'm still a child. I'm at school. The school is called The International School. *International means England plus some others.* All the teachers at my school are English or Scottish except for the French teacher who is French. I'm learning about things like William the Conqueror and The Battle of Hastings, 1066. I draw a picture of a Norman soldier and it fills a whole page. It's lunchtime. Everyone's outside playing. I had to stay inside because I spoke back to the teacher. She gave me lines to write out. *I must not ... I must not ...* After I finish my lines, I continue drawing the soldier. I work in his mail shirt, which reminds me of fish scales.

Soon I will be 37 years old. It's November 2007 and in London the clouds press downwards. In the mornings, the ceiling weighs heavily and the walls wobble. The flat in London is in the basement of a red-brick Victorian semi on the border of Hampstead and Golders Green. A narrow horizontal strip window in the bedroom lets in some light. Sometimes, I find snails crawling up the kitchen windows, which are set low down, almost at the level of the path outside. Clouds have found a way of getting into the room and into my head. The room smells of damp. Water clings to the windows and I draw shapes on the glass. Droplets sink deep into the timber frame, from which the paint is peeling off. I pick at the paint with a fingernail and then run my hand down the glass and shake the cold water from my fingers. I start going for walks. Every time I start out on a walk, I have to turn around and walk back. I have to walk back to check if the door really is locked and then I walk back to the pavement and turn left. The sky sits just above my head, off-white.

If I walk straight down the road, I won't get lost. I'll walk down and see where it ends and then I'll walk back.

I walk past rows of red-brick houses. Some of the tiles on the steps have come loose. Red geraniums are perched on a window sill and I look through the window, a light is on. Debris is piled up outside a house with scaffolding; men are fixing a roof. I hear an electric drill and a dog barking. I stop to see where it is, the barking dog, but it's nowhere to be seen. Then I see it, a fox terrier pushing its nose through a hedge. I walk a little further and Hampstead Heath comes into view in front of me. A wide muddy path stretches out with trees on either side. On my left, glimpses of brick through the trees and on my right there are trees as far as I can see. I look down at the wet mud, which is almost black. There are stones just below the surface along with twigs and sticks and leaves, scattered here and there, except at the edges where they lie thickly, in a long bank. Through the trees the sun is pale and I look right into it. The clouds have cleared and the sky is light blue. I walk off the path to a clearing. For the first time I see holly, not on Christmas cards or plastic replicas. A squirrel scuttles down a tree; it's swallowed by the leaves at the bottom of the trunk and then it disappears. I walk back onto the path which stretches out in front of me. I stop at a pond with water reflecting the clouds and the trees and even the colours of the leaves. I think of colours which describe the leaves and I think of russet apples. I think of silence and what it means now, in this place, which is new. The silence I'm thinking of is not silence in any literal sense. Rather, it's to do with peacefulness; the feeling of being settled in a body and a place. The feeling is ephemeral. It's there and then it's gone. My body is in London. But my mind is somewhere else. I am half in my body and half outside. I return to the Heath every day and I walk the same route. I tell myself that if I repeat the walk familiarity will yield a sense of belonging. But as I walk I realise that the belonging is not to any one place. My mind is restless. It travels between Seychelles, Johannesburg and then back to London. I try to stop it but I can't. Each time I walk the smell of the damp earth amongst the trees takes me back to the mountain.

Walking rearranges feelings. If I don't walk feelings

build up. I talk to myself in my head while I'm walking. I have conversations with people while I walk. The people I talk to are people I know, or have known. Some of them inhabit the past and some of them live in the present. As I walk, memories come flooding back. The memories are always the same and they repeat themselves over and over again. Things are happening. Things are happening in the world but they bounce right off.

I moved from Johannesburg to London with Nicholas. We were married in Johannesburg at the millennium. We said: 'We will never leave Johannesburg. This is home.' In Johannesburg everything came unstuck. No one was going to come out of centuries of violence unscathed. No one's going to come out of white supremacy unscathed. Scratch the surface. Scratch. Voices echo. They reverberate inside my head:

Don't look at me. I'm a good white. It's the Afrikaner. Who can argue with that? You think it was just us. Don't make me laugh. Look at the British. Look at what they did. They put my ancestors in concentration camps. Don't look at me. My ancestors fled persecution in Europe. Fuck you. My ancestors fled war. They fled hunger. That's how they came to South Africa. Don't look at me. I have black friends. I went to prison. I was in exile. Solid proof. Solid proof. Not me. I ducked the shrapnel. Oh come on it wasn't that bad. Anyway, nowadays they're all just reverse racists. And you know what some of them were helping out the State. Can you believe it? Killing their own people. Get a grip. Stop wallowing. Yesterday's news. And besides, things have changed. At the end of the day, we're all just human.

Guilt is feeling acutely bad for something you know you should never have done. You know you shouldn't have done it but you did it anyway. Once you realise you've been caught out, you might be angry. You might be furious with the person who caught you out. You will do anything to repress this sensation of guilt. You will do anything to make it go away. You might dream up reasons for why you shouldn't feel guilty. You might even bury the guilt. Perhaps you re-fashion the truth or deflect it somehow, even re-directing it back to the source. In these contortions you reveal something about yourself:

Sniff out the scapegoat. We appoint you. You will carry our shame, our fear, our madness, our loathing. If you speak out we will name you, we will dilute your concerns. It was only a joke. Don't be so sensitive. You sound unwell. Are you ok? Have you gone mad? We never said that. Give us proof. Give us evidence. We worry about you. We care about you. Until you get back to your senses we'll build an impenetrable stone wall to shield us from your madness. You'll beat at that wall with your fists until your knuckles bleed. But you won't even make a dent. Perhaps then you will curl your bleeding knuckles into a fist and

*beat someone. Beat them into a pulp. Or perhaps
you will jump off a building. Or perhaps you'll do
something. Do something with your life.*

The more vulnerable you appear to be, the more
you inhabit a space that can't be defined, delineated,
known, the more violence will find you. Violence
will find you because of your very being, your very
existence. Sometimes, violence will creep up on you
surreptitiously when you least expect it. There is the
violence that is enacted upon the body and there is
the violence that is enacted on the soul. Perhaps you
are invisible. You are invisible because you function
as a site of psychological projection. Perhaps you are
unseen because of how white supremacy has functioned across time and space, rendering you deficient.
But then this deficiency you have been made to feel
produces an unstoppable rage. The kind of rage
that is all-consuming. Perhaps you then also enact
violence. Or perhaps you have somehow transcended
your suffering and your anger. Perhaps you hold on
to forgiveness. If you don't hold onto forgiveness
you will go mad. Or the anger will eat you from the
inside out until you are all hollowed out. Until there
is nothing left. You might find a way to transcend
your humanness. Perhaps you can forgive. You can
forgive because that's what you were told to do in
church. Perhaps you can forgive the unforgiveable.
Perhaps there is something at stake or perhaps you
weren't given a choice. *Look, they say, the past is the
past. So, it happened. If you keep bringing it up we*

will stay there. We will stay there in the past. Then what? So what? Move on.

In Johannesburg, I taught an undergraduate course on the politics and ethics of visual images in South Africa. We would talk about the past knowing that each of us had a different relationship to it. One of my students told me: 'My uncle was an anti-apartheid activist. They put toxic stuff in his clothes, the damage is permanent. He hates whites. He hates them.' In South Africa, in the white academic spaces I inhabited, I experienced pressure to move on from the past, to speak of new things. But there is no line to be drawn between the past and the present. The past cannot simply be buried and forgotten about. The past lives on in the descendants of those who have suffered the kinds of things that don't just go away, the kinds of things that inhabit bodies and memories. Racism, xenophobia and prejudice in all of their iterations are not simply historical artefacts, inanimate objects. One day I will read a paragraph in a text by the South African scholar Premesh Lalu:'*Every year, colleagues report on the anxieties expressed by students as they struggle for a specifically South African idiom for speaking about being human. As a society, we have burdened our youth to find their way out of the ruins of apartheid. We also expect them to discover for themselves ways of thinking about the human condition, one that calls into question the claims of nineteenth and twentieth-century racisms.*'

I'm falling into an abyss. This abyss is a space without walls, without a floor. Perhaps if you suffer from depression you know that as you are falling into the abyss you are looking for something to hold onto but there is only nothingness. There is only darkness or you might imagine the abyss through other kinds of colours, images, sounds and textures. When I am deep inside this space I feel what might be described as the sensation of my soul leaving my body. I feel like a shell with everything scraped out of it. Sometimes the feeling is one that can only be described as pain except that the pain is not bodily, not physical, it is something for which there is no language. I long for nothingness; for a space without feeling, for an anaesthetic. In her book *Black Sun: Depression and Melancholia*, Julia Kristeva describes depression as a 'black sun': '*Out of which eerie galaxy do its invisible, lethargic rays reach me, pinning me to the ground, to my bed, compelling me to silence, to renunciation? … On the frontiers of life and death, occasionally I have the arrogant feeling of being witness to the meaninglessness of Being, of revealing the absurdity of bonds and beings.*'

I wake up with a feeling of tightness underneath my sternum. I take a breath. As I breathe in, I imagine my lungs filling up with air. I begin to panic as I think about the inside of my body. Organs and blood and damp and things I can't see. I feel as though I'm locked up inside a space so tiny it's impossible to stand up.

I can't breathe.
I close my eyes.
I imagine myself floating.
I'm floating on the surface of the sea.
The sea is warm.
I roll over in the water and pull myself downwards.
Beneath the surface there is sand and coral and
seaweed.
Fish dart in-between the coral and the seaweed.
The fish have black and white stripes.
Zebrafish.
Salty water burns my eyes.

I begin to fear what will happen if I don't find a way to activate my body, which is leaden and immovable. I begin to fear what will happen if I don't find a way to move from my bed to the door. I phone the Samaritans. The woman on the other end of the phone reminds me of my grandmother. She starts to talk to me. I can't see her. I can only hear her voice. She sounds older, much older than me; perhaps she's seen things I can't yet see. I close my eyes. I'm back in my grandmother's flat in Johannesburg. We're sitting at the dining room table drinking tea and eating rusks. I dip a rusk into my tea and put it into my mouth. It crumbles.

Just write. I don't know what to write. I open up a notebook and stare at the first page. The only things in my mind are memories. I begin to put them down. Memories suffused with rage. Sometimes I can't tell

78

one memory from another. Threads untangle. The more they untangle the more I write. Sometimes I write in a stream of consciousness. I write without stopping. Sometimes I make lists. I write about things I will reveal. And I write about things I will bury. I tear up the notebooks. I throw away the remains. I start a new book. I write down all my plans. The plans I write down promise new memories.

Black mould is creeping up the walls of the flat. I kneel down on the floor and touch the mould, which rubs off onto my fingers like a powder. I wash it off the wall. Each time it comes back I wash it off. I tell the landlord, who lives with his family in the house above the flat. 'Your fault', he says. 'Something you've done.' The relationship between the landlord and his family is claustrophobic. There is no sound insulation between the flat and the house and we can hear everything they do and say. Aside from the front door to our flat there is another leading from the landlord's house above. He uses this door to drop off our post. Whenever I hear the key in the lock I jump up. I'm always on edge. He can walk in at any time. If I'm there I leave whatever it is I'm doing and go up to the door. The flat shares utilities with the house. He calculates the cost and gives me bills in illegible, handwritten notes. The landlord responds to any problem with a shrug.

I set the table for dinner. Soon Nicholas will be home. I haven't spoken to anyone all day. I put on some music. I sing out loud and pour a glass of wine. I had slept all morning, drifting in and out of consciousness, dreaming of being somewhere else, childhood, floating in the sea, in the dusk, with the birds singing. It's January. By 4pm it's dark. The darkness wraps itself around me. I like it. I light candles. I turn on the heating. Someone is moving about in the house upstairs. I start to chop onions. I take another sip of wine. I'm back in Tante Hoppy's house. It's late in the afternoon. I hear conversations half in French and half in Creole, people stop and talk on the road outside. Tante Hoppy empties out a jar full of sweets from the local shop across the road. I choose the sherbet one. It's pastel coloured, pale pink. At the shop, where Hoppy buys the sweets, sacks of basmati rice are weighed out and carried home in pink and blue striped bags. Tonight, I'm cooking basmati from the corner shop down the road from my flat – fragrant rice with turmeric and star anise. I hold the star anise in the palm of my hand and breathe in its scent. I close my eyes.

Through the window of the flat, I can see a garden. I can see a lawn surrounded by flower beds and shrubs. We are not allowed to use it except when the family go on holiday. Once, when they were away, I went into the garden and walked around but I felt as though I was trespassing. In the summer, the garden comes to life, lush and scented. I open the windows to breathe it in. I see the landlord's wife trim back her plants or eat her lunch on the table outside. Once she started trimming a creeper outside my window. I asked her if she wanted a cup of tea but she shook her head and carried on trimming the creeper.

Before I left for London with Nicholas, we lived in a house in Johannesburg. We lived the life of white South Africans with access to a certain kind of historical privilege. When we moved into the house I said: 'I never want to leave this house. This is where we'll live forever.' The house was set high up on a ridge on the border between two suburbs in northern Johannesburg: Parktown West and Westcliff. These suburbs emerged out of the wealth generated by the gold-fields in late Victorian and Edwardian Johannesburg. Built in a colonial style reminiscent of the English architecture of the time, they also had substantial gardens, swimming pools and tree-lined streets. Our house, which was Edwardian, had a terraced garden. When we moved into it the garden was overgrown with ivy. I began to replant it with indigenous plants. The plants brought birds and butterflies to the garden and I was consumed by the walled-in, internal world I created. Of course, like all privileged South Africans we had the help of a gardener and a domestic worker. The property had a wall all around it with electric fencing and barbed wire. At night, we would lock all the doors, close all the windows and set the alarm. I was afraid of being raped. Stories of rape kept moving closer and closer until they brushed against my innermost circle.

Years before, in Johannesburg, I was travelling in a car with a friend. He was driving and I was in the passenger seat. It was a Saturday morning in a busy part of town. There was traffic all around us and it was moving slowly. A man on a motorbike pulled up close to my window and lifted up his shirt with one hand. A gun was lodged in his jeans. He looked into my eyes and he made me understand that he wanted something although what he wanted wasn't spoken. He stalked us down the road while we panicked and tried to get away. Then we swerved in front of a truck that had stopped at the side of the road. The man on the motorbike looked back at us and then he sped off.

I once heard a successful, white female professor articulate how bored she was by feminism and then I witnessed the applause. I never really understood what she meant particularly in a society within which the violence enacted upon women is so overt and so extreme. It was never clear to me that white South Africa had experienced an organised feminist movement of any significance. Women who were influential politically, culturally and intellectually appeared to be so through force of will, an unusual sense of agency and self-belief despite a deeply oppressive, patriarchal society. Perhaps it was that they were located in relation to unquestioned privilege or that they understood how to manipulate and navigate systems to their advantage. I have never personally experienced a feminist sense of community or belonging even though I subscribe to the ethics of feminism and its theorisation of what it means socially, politically and existentially to live as a being designated woman. The ethics of anti-racist thought and queer theory has opened up my understanding of what it continues to mean historically, socially, politically and philosophically to inhabit spaces labelled 'other' to an identified norm. Throughout my life there have been women who saw themselves as having a particular kind of status within South African society, a kind of assumed superiority and entitlement. After I was married there was a discernible shift in attitude towards me, a new respect, as if I had suddenly accrued some kind of social status. But I never wanted children. *I would never deprive my husband of a child', a woman in my social circle said to me. There was casualness to how she said it, a kind of easy entitlement.*

Ruth First was a journalist, academic and anti-apartheid activist who was killed by a letter bomb on the 17 August 1982 in Maputo, Mozambique. Her account of her arrest and interrogation in South Africa in 1963 was first published in 1965. I started reading the revised edition of her book, which was published in 2006, the year before I left Johannesburg. *'To see through the larger window I had to stand on tiptoe on the iron bedstead and hang from the bars of my cage. Immediately under the window was the main road of the Prison Department estate and across the way – mocking my incarceration – stretched a splendid swimming pool, complete with high diving*

board and trampoline, lawns and flower gardens,
and further afield but still well within my view, two
bowling greens and several tennis courts. These
were the recreation grounds of the (white) Prisons
Department staff and their families ... I was appalled
at the events of the last three days. They had beaten
me. I had allowed myself to be beaten. I had pulled
back from the brink just in time, but had it been in
time?'

There's a party somewhere on a rooftop in North
London; South Africans and Zimbabweans are
here. Miles Davis. We're sitting around a table and
we're drinking and talking about politics. One of the
Zimbabweans looks at me. I watch as his eyes pause
on my leopard print shoes. I notice a half-smile;
something is amusing him. We start talking about
South Africa. The more I talk the more I feel the now
familiar sensation of anxiety heighten. I know my face
is flushed and my heart is beating faster. The redness
makes me more anxious; exposed. The more anxious
I become the more I talk without censoring myself.
He says: 'You know what. You know what I think?
I think white South Africans are also traumatised.
Yes. They're also traumatised.' I wonder where his
benevolence comes from. After all, he is black and I
am white. Someone else says. 'South Africans need
to move on. Stuck in the past. That's what they
are. Apartheid. That's their big thing. Their claim
to fame.' *Laughter*. I feel my stomach tighten. It
tightens up into a fist. I get up. I walk to the kitchen.

Someone's standing next to the kitchen sink. I look at him and I smile. He asks: 'South African?' 'Yes, well half.' I ask: 'Where are you from?' *He snaps.* 'Why do you need to know where I'm from?' Pause. 'Can we not have another kind of conversation?' *I snap.* 'You asked me where *I* was from first!' 'I didn't' 'Yes. You did. You're making assumptions about me.' Now we're arguing back and forth: a black man and a white woman. Another man joins in. 'Do you know anything about ideology?' he asks. My heart is pounding and I'm angry. I'm more than angry, I'm furious. I feel their condescension. I feel what it feels like to be a woman being told off by a man. I feel that familiar feeling of a man explaining things to me. The host hears us arguing and he's worried. My voice gets louder and louder. 'Please. Stop. For me!' The host pleads. But I can't stop. I can't stop. 'You're assuming things about me.' 'What am I assuming?' 'You know very well what you're assuming.' 'No I don't.' I turn around and walk away and then I hear it: 'Bitch.'

Where are you from? The question is not innocent and that night at the party on the rooftop I had thrown it into the air. I had forgotten to think about my words and how it is I deliver them and to whom. I had forgotten that I was a white South African woman talking to a black Zimbabwean man. Perhaps he had made up his mind about me before I had even opened my mouth. Perhaps I was wilful in my refusal of the fact of his blackness and the fact of my whiteness. In the years following the fight with the man at the party, I find this question in the books I start to read. The books teach me about racism in Britain, about histories of migration from the countries that once constituted the British Empire and a tenuous idea of Britishness and belonging. I make a list and I title it 'Where are you from?'

Stuart Hall, *Familiar Stranger*, published in 2017. '*As I explained, much of this turned on my reflections on how to answer the innocent – or not so innocent – question: "Where are you from?" For all its apparent simplicity, it's heavily loaded. I'm reminded of James Baldwin encountering a West Indian at the British Museum in the 1960s, and his being confronted by just this question. "Where are you from?" Even after Baldwin had set out his origins as clearly as he knew how – "I was born in Harlem General Hospital" – his interlocutor persisted, until he finally posed Baldwin the question: "But where were you born before that?"*'

Sara Ahmed, *Living a Feminist Life*, published in 2017. '*To be asked 'Where are you from?' is a way of being told you are not from here. The questioning, the interrogation, can only stop when you have explained yourself. For me to explain myself, to explain where I am from, is not only to give an account of not being from here (being from Australia as not being from here would not suffice; that I am born here in the United Kingdom would not suffice), it is an account of how I ended up brown. Brownness is registered as foreign; brown as elsewhere.*'

Afua Hirsch, *Brit(ish)*, published in 2018. *'But being asked where you're from in your own country is a daily ritual of unsettling.'*

When I asked the black Zimbabwean man the question 'Where are you from?' worded in a specific way, I ignited something historical, something political. History put a stop to our conversation before it even began. In that moment, I was white and he was black. Even though we were both born on the African continent I will always be linked to the figure of the white oppressor. This is an inescapable fact. I will never escape this history. I don't know why he migrated to London but in this other place his blackness and my whiteness take on other inflections. These inflections have to do with who is seen to belong and who is not. On several occasions white British people have said to me: 'You're the kind of immigrant we want' in the same breath as racist sentiments are expressed.

I'm in the sea
The water's crystal clear
I can see the sand below, just white sand, no sea-
weed
I lie on my back and close my eyes
The sun is intense
It burns my skin
Something stings my arm
Jelly fish float in the water around me
Translucent

I'm looking at the edges of a pond on Hampstead Heath. I look at the black soil and the leaves and the twigs. Then, I focus on the pond itself. I look downwards into the water. The water is dark and you cannot see into its depths. The surface of the water ripples in the breeze. The ripple is so subtle that you might not notice it at all. A tree is reflected in the water. The reflected tree appears to have three trunks that extend upwards from a base. I discover that one of the trunks belongs to another tree. The tree is leafless, stark, and its branches reach down into the depths of the water. For a moment, I hear nothing but silence. The silence reverberates inside my head. After today there will be tomorrow and then the day after that and the day after that. I hear a crow. *Caw. Caw. Caw. Caw.* Behind me, footsteps crunch through twigs and leaves. Behind the footsteps, faster ones, a dog. Sounds move closer and then further and then closer again. It's getting dark. Through the trees I see the lights of cars and then a bus, glimpses of red. As it gets darker it gets colder. I feel the cold on my skin. I feel it through my coat. I walk back on the path and as I walk memories overlay, mutable, they shift and then they transform.

Library

Hazel de Silva, '*Madame* Blanche', *Sega of Seychelles* (Nairobi, Kenya: East African Publishing House Ltd, 1983) p.169 and p.170; 'The island of torment', p.236.

Bernard Georges, *The Fortunate Islands: Gossip from the Seychelles* (Seychelles: Calusa Bay Publications, 2011). The points about the numbers of islands that make up the Seychelles archipelago is taken from p.7. The anecdote about the statue of Queen Victoria is from p.110.

William McAteer, *Hard Times in Paradise: The History of Seychelles 1827–1919* (Mahé, Seychelles: Pristine Books) p.xii.

References to the Creole language are drawn from Julien Durup, *The Seychelles Islands and its First Landowners 1786–1833* (Seychelles: iMedia, 2013) p.32. I am also indebted to this book for its historical account and archival research more generally.

References to the Afrikaans language are from 'Afrikaans: The Language of Black and Coloured Dissent', published on the on-line historical and archival platform *South African History Online: Towards a People's History* www.sahistory.org.za/article/ afrikaans-language-black-and-coloured-dissent (last accessed: 10 July 2019).

Zimitri Erasmus, 'Re-imagining coloured identities in post-Apartheid South Africa'. In Zimitri Erasmus (ed.), *Coloured by History, Shaped by Place: New Perspectives on Coloured Identities in Cape Town* (South Africa: Kwela Books and SA History Online, 2001) p.13.

Ngũgĩ wa Thiong'o, *Decolonising the Mind: The Politics of Language in African Literature* (London: James Currey; Nairobi: Heinemann Kenya; Portsmouth N.H.: Heinemann; Harare: Zimbabwe Publishing House, 1986) p.11.

Jean Rhys, *Smile Please: An Unfinished Autobiography* (first published by André Deutsch Ltd, 1979; my edition published by Penguin/Random House, UK, 1990 and reissued in 2016) p.7.

'Bessie Amelia Head', published on South African History Online www.sahistory.org.za/people/bessie-amelia-head (last accessed: 11 July 2019).

Bessie Head, *Maru* (Oxford: Heinemann International, 1987) p.11.

Percy Mtwa, Mbongeni Ngema and Barney Simon, *Woza Albert!* (London: Methuen Drama, 1983).

Pumla Gqola, 'Defining people: Analysing power, language and representation in metaphors of the New South Africa', *Transformation* 47 (2001), pp.94–106 and p.100.

The paragraph on Vlakplaas and the case of Sizwe Kondile is drawn from my PhD dissertation, Yvette Greslé, *Precarious Video: Historical events, trauma and memory in South African video art – Jo Ractliffe, Penny Siopis, Berni Searle and Minnette Vári* (London: University College London, 2015) p.85.

Njabulo Ndebele, *South African Literature and Culture: Rediscovery of the Ordinary* (Manchester and New York: Manchester University Press, 2006).

Frantz Fanon, *Black Skin, White Masks*, translated from the French by Charles Lam Markmann (New York: Grove Press, 1967) p.12 and p.116.

Steve Biko, *I Write What I Like* (South Africa: Picador Africa, an imprint of Pan Macmillan, South Africa, 2004) p.163 and p.2.

Winnie Madikizela-Mandela, *91 Days: Prisoner Number 1323/69* (South Africa: Picador Africa, 2013, 2017) p.5 and p.10.

Akil K. Khalfani and Tukufu Zuberi, 'Racial classification and the modern census in South Africa, 1911–1996', *Race and Society* 4 (2001) pp.161–176.

Simonne Horwitz, *Baragwanath Hospital, Soweto: A History of Medical Care 1941–1990* (Johannesburg: Wits University Press, 2013).

'Thembisile Chris Hani', published on South African History Online www.sahistory.org.za/people/thembisile-chris-hani (last accessed: 11 July 2019).

Premesh Lalu, 'Still searching for "the human"', *Social Dynamics: A Journal of African Studies*, 38:1, 2012, pp.3–7, p.5.

Julia Kristeva, *Black Sun: Depression and Melancholia*, translated from the French by Leon S. Roudiez (New York: Columbia University Press, 1989) pp.3 and 4.

Ruth First, *117 Days: An account of confinement and interrogation under the South African 90-Day Detention Law* (South Africa: Penguin Books, 2006) pp.56 and 122.

Stuart Hall, *Familiar Stranger: A Life Between Two Islands* (United Kingdom: Allen Lane, an imprint of Penguin Books, 2017) p.95.

Sara Ahmed, *Living a Feminist Life* (Durham and London: Duke University Press, 2017) pp.116–117.

Afua Hirsch, *Brit(ish): On Race, Identity and Belonging* (London: Jonathan Cape, 2018) p.33.

Future Editions

For future editions, please visit the Copy Press website

Copy Press is committed to bringing readers and writers together and invites you to join its Reader's Union – please visit www.copypress.co.uk